NEW ANATOMIES

by
TIMBERLAKE WERTENBAKER

D1519365

The Dramatic Publishing Company
Woodstock, Illinois • London, England • Melbourne, Australia

NEW ANATOMIES

A Full Length Play
For Five Women and a Musician
(The roles are distributed as follows:)

CHARACTERS

1. ISABELLE EBERHARDT and, in her Arab persona,
                                                SI MAHMOUD
2. SEVERINE / ANTOINE / BOU SAADI
3. NATALIE / EUGENIE / MURDERER / JUDGE
4. JENNY / SALEH / LYDIA / COLONEL LYAUTEY
5. VERDA MILES / ANNA / SI LACHMI / YASMINA
   CAPTAIN SOUBIEL

THE TIME: The turn of the century.

THE PLACE: Europe and Algeria.

A Note On The Staging

The role of PASHA (Act Two Scene One) is silent, and should be taken by the musician.

Except for the actress playing ISABELLE, each actress plays a Western woman, an Arab man and a Western man. Changes should take place in such a way as to be visible to the audience and all five actresses should be on stage at all times.

The songs in the play ought to be popular music-hall songs from the turn of the century. Songs 2 and 3 belong to the repertoire of the male impersonator, and Song 1 to that of the *ingénue.* The songs, except for the one beginning Act Two, are optional.

T. W.

ACT ONE

SCENE ONE

Ain-Sefra, a dusty village in Algeria. ISABELLE EBERHARDT looks around, none too steady. She is dressed in a tattered Arab cloak, has no teeth and almost no hair. She is twenty-seven.

ISABELLE. Lost the way. *(Steadies herself.)* Detour. Closed. *(Pause. As if an order to herself.)* Go inside. *(Sings, softly, Arabic modulations, but flat:)* "If a man be old and a fool, his folly..." *(Burps.)* That's what it is. *(Takes out a cigarette and looks for a match through the folds of her cloak.)* Match. *(Forgets about it. Sings:)* "If a man be old and a fool, his folly is past all cure. But a young man..." What it is is this: *(Looks around.)* I need a fuck. *(Pause.)* Definitely. Yes.

(SEVERINE enters. She is a slightly older woman, dressed uncomfortably for the heat in a long skirt and jacket.)

ISABELLE. Trailed...*(To SEVERINE.)* Trailing behind me.
SEVERINE. Come inside.
ISABELLE. Inside? Trailed: the story, I know. Stealing it.
SEVERINE. You have a fever. *(ISABELLE remembers her cigarette.)*
ISABELLE. Matches. Stolen. *(Louder.)* You stole my matches. *(SEVERINE finds the matches, tries to light*

ISABELLE's cigarette. Apologetic.) Desert wind: makes the hand shake. *(SEVERINE lights two cigarettes and sticks one in ISABELLE's mouth.)* Pay for my story with a match. European coinage!

SEVERINE. You need rest.

ISABELLE. No, later. *(Burps.)* Found out what it was. What was it? Ah, yes. It was: I need a fuck. I need a fuck. Where am I going to find a fuck? Bunch of degenerates in this town. Sleeping WHEN I NEED A FUCK. It's the European influence. Keeps them down.

SEVERINE. Come inside, Isabelle.

ISABELLE. "Please go inside, mademoiselle, and stay there." Out of the wind. Saw a couple of guards earlier. That'll do. One for you, one for me. I'll give you the younger one, rules of hospitality. No? Sevvy the scribe prefers a belly dancer, eh, dark smooth limbs and curved hips. Or the voluptuous tale. Your face looks like a big, hungry, European cock. No offense: not your fault you look European. Must find those guards. *(Stares.)* Coolness of the night as it filters through the sand. The smell of sand, Severine, do you know it? It's like the inside of water. Smell…*(She leans down and falls flat.)*

SEVERINE. Isabelle, please…*(They struggle to get her up.)*

ISABELLE. You going to write I couldn't walk straight enough to find a fuck? They'll want to know everything. I'm famous now, not just anybody, no, I'll be in History. *(Near retch.)* They hate me, but I forgive them. You tell them…that when the body drags through the gutter, it is cleaved from the soul. Tell them the soul paced the desert. They take baths, but lice crawl through the cracks of their hypocritical brains. Bunch of farmers. Wallowing in the mud of their plowed fields. Turnips, cabbages, carrots, all in a line, all fenced in. *(Cries.)* Why do they hate me so? I didn't want anything from them. *(Pause.)* Si Mahmoud forgives all. Si Mahmoud paced the desert. Heart unmixed with guile, free. Why aren't you writing all this down, chronicler? Duty to get it right, no editing. *(Burps.)* Edit that.

SEVERINE. Please, Si Mahmoud. Let's go in.

ISABELLE. Listen. The dawn's coming. You can tell by the sound, a curve in the silence and then the sand in the desert moves...Write down: a third of a centimetre, they'll want to know that in Europe. *(Pause. SEVERINE, resigned, sits with ISABELLE.)* When I was growing up in the Tsar's villa in St. Petersburg...

SEVERINE. Geneva.

ISABELLE. What?

SEVERINE. You said Geneva earlier.

ISABELLE. Did I? Yes, ducks...must have been Geneva.

SEVERINE *(delicately)*. Your brothers...

ISABELLE. Didn't have any.

SEVERINE. You said...

ISABELLE. I was the only boy in the family.

SEVERINE. Your brother Antoine...

ISABELLE. Beloved. *(Makes a gesture for fucking.)* Didn't. Would have. Nasty little piece got her claws in him first. No, did.

SEVERINE. Si Mahmoud, the truth.

ISABELLE. There is no god but Allah, Allah is the only God and Muhammed is his prophet.

SEVERINE. What brought you to the desert? *(ISABELLE makes a trace on the ground.)* It's in Arabic.

ISABELLE *(reads)*. The Mektoub: it was written. Here. That means, no choice. Mektoub.

SEVERINE. Your mother?

ISABELLE. No choice for her either. The Mektoub.

SEVERINE. You told me she was a delicate woman. What gave her the courage to run off?

ISABELLE. Even the violet resists domestication.

SEVERINE. But in the 1870s...

ISABELLE. Severine, it is a courtesy in this country not to interrupt or ask questions of the storyteller. You must sit quietly and listen, moving only to light my cigarettes. When I pause, you may praise Allah for having given my tongue such vivid modulations. I shall begin, as is our custom, with a mention of women.

SONG I

VERDA MILES as a Victorian girl in frills.

SCENE TWO

Geneva. A house in disorder. VERDA MILES takes off her ribbons, puts up her hair and covers herself with a shawl, becoming ANNA, a woman in her late thirties, with remnants of style and charm.

ANNA. And then the children...They won't stay.

(ISABELLE and ANTOINE appear. ISABELLE is thirteen, dressed in a man's shirt and a skirt much too big for her. ANTOINE is sixteen, frail and feminine.)

ISABELLE. Antoine, Antoine. Don't let him frighten you.

ANTOINE *(near tears)*. Drunken tyrant.

ISABELLE. Let's dream.

ANTOINE. He threatened to hit me. Brute. I have to go away, now.

ANNA *(paying no attention to any of this)*. First Nicholas, not a word...He must have come to a bad...Too many anarchists in the house. It's a bad influence on children.

ISABELLE. Oh yes, let's go away. We're in Siberia. The snow is up to our knees, so hard to move. Suddenly, look, shining in the dark, a pair of yellow eyes.

ANTOINE. I have no choice. I'll have to run away and join the army.

ISABELLE. I'll come with you, we can take Mama.

ANTOINE. The army's only for boys.

ISABELLE. We can't leave Mama.

ANTOINE. I wish I was a girl. He doesn't treat you that way.

ISABELLE. I'm strong.

ANTOINE. He'll kill me.

ANNA. If only Trofimovitch had allowed some fairy tales, even Pushkin...not all these Bakunin pamphlets at bedtime.

ISABELLE. It's snowing again. Darkness. Another pair of yellow eyes, glistening. Another. We're surrounded. Are they wolves?

ANTOINE *(joining in reluctantly)*. No, those are the eyes of our enemies.

ISABELLE. You're shivering.

ANNA. And now Natalie...

ANTOINE. I'm cold. It's too cold up there. I want to go further south.

ISABELLE. The Crimea, lemon groves.

ANTOINE. "Knowst thou the land, beloved, where the lemons bloom..." No, I want to go further south. Far away. The Sahara.

ANNA. And Natalie's so good with...

ISABELLE. Our camels are tired.

ANTOINE. That's the sort of thing Natalie would say.

ISABELLE *(offended)*. The transition from Siberia was too sudden. I haven't acclimatated.

ANTOINE. Acclimatized.

ANNA. It's all so difficult. *(Flute music.)*

ISABELLE. This stillness.

ANTOINE. Dune after dune, shape mirroring shape, so life...weariness.

ISABELLE. How rapidly the sun seems to plunge behind the dunes. This stillness.

ANTOINE. Let us rest, my beloved.

ISABELLE. I'll build our tent. There's a storm coming, I can see the clouds.

ANTOINE. There aren't any clouds over the desert.

ISABELLE. That's what Natalie would say.

ANTOINE. You don't understand, the corners of a dream must be nailed to the ground as firmly as our tent: no rain in the desert.

ISABELLE. A wind then. Listen, the wind's galloping over the dunes.

ANTOINE. It's a sandstorm.

ISABELLE. Quick. Where are you? I can't see you.

ANTOINE. Here, come here, my beloved. *(They throw themselves into each other's arms, roll on the floor.)* Beloved. *(Their embrace lingers.)*

ANNA. Natalie mustn't...she's too good with *(Notices the two children.)* Antoine, I'm not sure you should...with your sister...like that.

ISABELLE. We're playing, Mama, we're dreaming.

ANNA. Are you too old? I don't know. The poets...But Natalie...

ANTOINE. Wants us to behave—

ISABELLE. Like Swiss clocks. Tick tock.

ANTOINE. Tick tock.

ANNA. You mustn't...She is sometimes a little...but she's the only one, she's so good with dust. I don't seem to manage very well. There's so much of it and it's complicated finding it. I wasn't brought up to...But this new world of Trofimovitch, where it's wrong to have servants, well yes, but what about the dust? I suppose when the revolution comes, they'll find a way, deal with it.

ISABELLE. We don't mind.

ANNA. Natalie...wants to leave us.

ANTOINE. Even Natalie can't take the beast any more.

ANNA. Isabelle, she's always been very fond...Tell her she absolutely mustn't...

ISABELLE. She's free.

ANNA. But Trofimovitch...

(NATALIE enters. She is a tightly pulled together young woman. An awkward silence and a sense that this is not unusual when she comes into a room.)

ANNA. Natalie, I was saying...to abandon your home...

NATALIE. How can you call this pigsty a home?

ANNA. Darling, a young lady's vocabulary shouldn't include...Your family...

NATALIE. Family. *(Looks around at them.)* In a family you have first a mother who looks after her children, protects them, teaches them...

ANNA. Didn't I? You knew several poems of Byron as a child.

NATALIE. A mother who teaches her children how to behave and looks after the house, cooks meals, doesn't let
her children eat out of a slop bucket—

ANNA. Trofimovitch says meals are a bourgeois form
of...But don't we have...

NATALIE. When I cook them. And secondly in a family
a brother is a brother, a boy then a man, not this snivelling, delicate half girl. You've allowed him to be terror-
ized by that drunken beast.

ANNA. Natalie, his mind, philosophy...

NATALIE. Philosophy, don't make me laugh. Yes, and
finally in a family you have a proper father, not that
raving peasant, who's driven us to this misery and filth,
who's now trying to get into my bed at night.

ANNA. He's not always very steady at night, he must
have thought...He didn't notice it wasn't his...

NATALIE (exploding). And you defend him. My mother
defends the man who's ruining all of us, you defend the
man who's trying to seduce your own daughter. You
won't leave that filthy lecherous drunk, you prefer to
ruin us.

ANNA. Leave him...go...where?

ISABELLE. Natalie, love forgives.

NATALIE. Love, that spittle of stinking brandy. Love?

ISABELLE (gently). "Love has its reasons...

ANTOINE. ...which reason cannot fathom."

NATALIE. The two of you with your books!

ANNA (feebly). Isabelle is right...She doesn't mind...

NATALIE. At her age you love anybody, even beggars,
even a snivelling brother. (To ISABELLE.) I'll come
back and get you later, then you can come live with me
in a real home, with a real family, with my husband.

ISABELLE. A husband, Natalie. That's different. Is he dark? Is he foreign? Does he visit you only at night and wrap you in a blinding veil of torrid passion? A secret husband, how wonderful, like Eros and Psyche. Does he let you look at him?

NATALIE. What are you talking about? I'm marrying Stéphane.

ANTOINE. Stéphane, the shopkeeping weed. He's driven you to that?

NATALIE. You're one to talk, you fine figure of manhood.

ISABELLE. He does look like a dandelion, you said so yourself.

NATALIE. He'll soon be my husband and I'll have him talked about with respect. We'll be very happy.

ISABELLE. How? If he knows you don't love him.

NATALIE. Love, look where that got us. Oh, I tell him I love him, men like to hear that, sometimes I tell him I adore him.

ANNA. To lie...I'm not sure...

NATALIE. I can't have you at the wedding. I explained he was too ill. Stéphane's family's a little upset I'm foreign. But they'll see, I'll make a wonderful home for him. *(Pause.)* I must get my things. Don't tell him, it won't do any good. *(She leaves.)*

ANNA. I don't understand, what have I done? But you, my babies, you'll never leave, no, you couldn't now. What did you say, Isabelle? Torrid passion, yes, I think, with Trofimovitch, it was...He was so strong, so convinced, impossible to think clearly...And then, how wrong it was to have servants, husband, hypocrisy of the sacrament, he said, and how my life made millions suffer. Would you have preferred a big house? You see, there are so many rules when you...The doctor says a frail heart...There's no choice when your heart is... *(She drifts off.)*

ISABELLE. At last the silence descends on the darkening dunes. How still is our solitude, my beloved, how still the desert.

ANTOINE. Let's stop here.

ISABELLE. Yes, let's grow old together and watch the hours stretch on the ground.

ANTOINE *(moving away)*. Beloved, forgive me, but I must.

ISABELLE. I can't see you. You sound so far away.

ANTOINE. I don't have the strength any more, forgive me...

ISABELLE. Where have you gone? Oh, please. Abandoned, alas, nothing to do.

ANTOINE *(from off)*. But wait.

ISABELLE. Wait...and all around me, death. *(Screams.)* Dead.

SCENE THREE

Geneva, a few years later. NATALIE and ISABELLE.

NATALIE. Dead?

ISABELLE. Dead. Both of them. Mama first, almost immediately after she received Antoine's letter. It broke her heart, those years of silence, not knowing, her frail heart. And then the letter from the Legion! Antoine a Legionnaire, he'll never survive.

NATALIE. It might be just the thing for him. Turn him into a man.

ISABELLE. He didn't even tell me, the coward, the traitor. He must have planned it for months in secret. And then a cool letter describing life in the barracks and, now, marriage. I'll have to find him before it's too late.

NATALIE. And him? Drank himself to death?

ISABELLE. Poor Trofimovitch. He'd begun to put his ear to the ground listening for the sound of the revolution. He said he'd hear it when it came, he still had the ear of a Russian peasant. And he despaired of the silence. When Mama died, he...turned and twisted, crumpled himself into a knot and kept his ear to the floor, but this time I think he was listening for her. "Three be the ways of love: a knitting of heart to heart—that's Antoine and me—a pleasing of lips and eyes, and a third love whose name is death." That's Trofimovitch and Mama. It's from an Arabic poem. Trofimovitch taught it to me. There's a similar one in Greek...

NATALIE. Mama should have taught you to sweep instead. If I'd learnt properly when I was young my mother-in-law wouldn't have found so much to complain about. But Stéphane has been very patient. I'm lucky. *(Takes in the disorder.)* We can start on this house. Stéphane thinks we'll get a lot of money for it, sell it to some English aristocrats. They like these gloomy old places.

ISABELLE. The house belongs to Antoine. He'll want to come back here and live with me.

NATALIE. He'll want his own little home now.

ISABELLE. "And the screen of separation was placed between us."

NATALIE. The house belongs to all of us. Your share of the money can help towards the expense of having you live with us, and you'll have some left over for your marriage. I wish I'd been able to bring some to my husband, although he never reproached me.

ISABELLE. What's marriage like?

NATALIE. We're doing very well with the shop now and soon we'll build our own house, a big one.

ISABELLE. I mean at night.

NATALIE. You get used to it.

ISABELLE. Brutal pain and brutal pleasure, and after, languor. "And the breeze languished in the evening hours as if it had pity for me."

NATALIE. You've been reading too much. You mustn't talk like that to men. When they come into the shop you must be seen working very hard, dusting things very carefully. That always inspires young men. We've thought a lot about Stéphane's cousin. He has a flower shop and he won't mind the fact that you look so strong. You could help him in the garden. You'd like that.

ISABELLE. Does he grow cactus plants?

NATALIE. They're the wrong plants for this climate.

ISABELLE. It's the wrong climate for the plants. I'm going to Algeria.

NATALIE. The thought of marriage frightened me too, but I'll help you make a good choice. You'll need a roof over your head.

ISABELLE. No rain in the desert, no need for a roof.

NATALIE. We're in Geneva and I'm here to protect you until you're safely married.

ISABELLE. Geneva of the barred horizons. I'm getting out, I need a gallop on the dunes.

NATALIE. You'll forget all that when you're married. You'll forget all those dreams.

ISABELLE *(looking at NATALIE for the first time)*. Poor Natalie, left the dreams to look for order, but order was not happiness.

NATALIE. You always made fun of me, you and Antoine, but I always cared for you and I'm determined to help you. When you understand what life is like without the books, you'll understand me, you'll see.

ISABELLE. Geneva to Marseilles by train, Marseilles to Algiers by boat and then a camel for the desert.

NATALIE. That's enough now. It's your duty.

ISABELLE. Words of a Swiss preacher, song of the rain on the cultivated fields.

NATALIE. You have to obey me. You have no choice.

ISABELLE. Trofimovitch told me obedience comes not from direct fear, but fear of the rules. I have no fear, he always said I was the bravest.

NATALIE. He had no right to treat you as if you were an exception. *(Pause.)* You're still so young, we won't force you. We'll give you a year, even more. *(Silence.)* If we sell this house, we can take a little trip to Algeria. I want to see what they have over there. They say Arabs are very stupid and give you valuable jewels and clothes for trinkets. Will you agree to that?

ISABELLE. The desert.

NATALIE. Stéphane's arranging the papers for the house and then he'll get us all passports. You couldn't get one by yourself.

ISABELLE. Antoine, we'll gallop over the desert.

NATALIE. I'll be so pleased to sell this house. All buried at last.

ISABELLE. Antoine!

SCENE FOUR

Algiers. ANTOINE in a crumpled civil service suit sits smoking, tired, grey. JENNY, young and very pregnant, is bustling. ISABELLE is staring out and YASMINA, a servant, is polishing something, extremely slowly.

JENNY *(to ANTOINE)*. Why doesn't your sister ever help? She hasn't lifted a finger since she's been here. She talks too much to the servant. I have enough trouble making that woman work. They're so lazy, these people. She's said more to that girl than to me. Call her over, Antoine. She never listens when I talk to her.

ANTOINE *(weakly)*. Isabelle. *(ISABELLE turns.)*

JENNY. Please remember that Fatma is a native and a servant. They don't respect you if you treat them...

ISABELLE. Her name isn't Fatma.

JENNY. Their names are unpronounceable. We call them all Fatma.

ISABELLE. Her name is beautiful: Yasmina. Poor girl, they tried to marry her to a cousin she hated. It was death or the degradation of becoming a servant. I'll write about her.

JENNY. I wouldn't believe anything she says. Help me polish some glasses. I can't trust Fatma with them.

ISABELLE. Throw over a cigarette, will you, Antoine.

JENNY. Women shouldn't smoke. It makes them look vulgar, doesn't it, Antoine?

ISABELLE. Matches.

JENNY. And you work very hard for your cigarettes. They don't grow on trees. Some people have to pay for everything and soon we'll have another mouth to feed.

ANTOINE. Isabelle'll help us when she sells some articles.

JENNY. She won't sell any by just sitting around smoking.

ISABELLE. Inspiration doesn't come frying potatoes. *(ANTOINE laughs.)*

JENNY. You always take her side. You don't care what happens to me. She hasn't even offered to knit something for the baby.

ISABELLE *(bored)*. Yasmina will help me find something.

JENNY. I'm not going to put some horrible native cloth around my beautiful new baby.

ISABELLE. I'll get Natalie to send you my collection of poems when she goes back. Do you remember that beautiful one of Lermontov Mama used to recite, about the young soul crying out its entrapment in the womb? The dumb joy of the mother but for "a long time it languished in the world, filled with a wonderful longing and earth's tedious songs..." how does it go?

ANTOINE *(awkward)*. I don't remember.

ISABELLE. "Could not drown out the last sounds of Paradise..."

JENNY. You're jealous, that's all, because you can't find a husband. Natalie told me how you frightened Stéphane's cousin away.

ISABELLE. He looked like an orchid.

ANTOINE. You're worse than Arabs, you two, fighting about nothing.

ISABELLE. Is that what they teach you in the barracks?

JENNY. He's not in the barracks any more. He has a very good job.

ISABELLE. Sitting on your bum, staring at numbers.

JENNY. And he'll be promoted soon.

ISABELLE. To longer numbers.

JENNY. If you don't ruin his chances. You've been heard talking to the natives in their own language. There's no reason not to talk to them in French.

ISABELLE *(to ANTOINE)*. You hate it, don't you, this life?

JENNY. People are becoming suspicious. This is a small community.

ISABELLE. Tick tock, a Swiss clock, the needle that crushes the dreams to sleep.

JENNY. You think food just appears on the table. It has to be paid for.

ISABELLE. And only ten miles from the desert. You might as well have stayed in Switzerland for all you've seen of it.

ANTOINE. I did see it. It's not how we dreamt of it. It's dangerous, uncomfortable, and most of it isn't even sand.

ISABELLE. Freedom.

JENNY. Life is much cheaper here than in Switzerland. We'll go back when we have enough money to buy a decent house.

ISABELLE. "Oh the bitter grief of never again exchanging one single thought." Remember how we knew all of Loti by heart and we dreamt of moving, always moving.

ANTOINE. Life isn't what we dreamed.

ISABELLE. It could be...the rolling movement of camels, movement, Antoine.

JENNY. Rolling stone gathers no moss. I don't want my baby to be poor.

ISABELLE. Remember when we followed the Berber car-
avan and we had the sandstorm, oh, my beloved...

ANTOINE. I saw the Berbers. One wrong move and they
slit your throat. They don't like Europeans.

ISABELLE. Not Europeans with guns, but we could talk
to them. Freedom.

JENNY. You keep talking as if Antoine was a slave. He
has a good job. We'll be able to take holidays, have a
house. That's freedom: money.

ANTOINE. I see how things are now.

ISABELLE. What dictionary are you using? The Swiss
clockmaker's or the poet's? *(An Arabic flute, offstage.)*
Or his? Listen. I hear him every evening, but I've never
seen him come or go. He's just there, suddenly, calling.

JENNY. It's probably a beggar and he'll come asking for
money. Chase him away, Antoine. They carry diseases
these people. It's bad for the baby. *(They ignore her.
She shouts.)* Go away, you savage, go away, go away!
(Silence. Embarrassed.) I'm so tired and nervous. This
isn't a friendly country. It's not easy to have a baby. It
doesn't happen all by itself.

(NATALIE enters, arms full of materials and clothes.)

NATALIE. It's wonderful how stupid these people are.
They give you things for nothing.

ISABELLE. The word is generosity, gifts of hospitality.

NATALIE. Look at this one, it's worth a fortune, that em-
broidery, that detail. They're terribly clever for savages.
Look at this woman's cloak.

ISABELLE. It's not for a woman.

NATALIE. We'll be the first shop in Switzerland to sell
these oriental things. They're all the rage in Paris. You

could even model some of them, Isabelle. Here's a woman's dancing costume.

JENNY. Give it to me.

NATALIE. I can't wait to get back. We'll make a fortune.

ISABELLE. I'm not coming back with you.

NATALIE. Nonsense. *(NATALIE continues to lay out the clothes. JENNY wraps her face in a veil.)*

JENNY. I'm in your harem. You're the sheikh. Oh, come to me.

ANTOINE. You look grotesque.

JENNY. You're so cruel. I'll hide behind my veil.

ISABELLE. That's not a woman's veil. Women in the desert don't wear veils, only the Tuareg men do. *(She starts dressing JENNY.)* It should be wrapped around the head and worn with this. This is called a jellaba. It can be worn in any kind of weather. The hood will protect you against the elements, or against the enemy. It's very useful for warriors.

JENNY. I don't want to be dressed as a man.

ISABELLE. Why not? The baby might end up looking like an Arab? He'll run away from you into the desert.

NATALIE. You look lovely. Don't tease her, Isabelle. When you're pregnant you have these caprices. I couldn't wear red or walk into the house without making three turns in the garden.

ANTOINE. It's like the Arabs. They'll never do anything without going through fifty useless gestures.

ISABELLE. The word is courtesy. *(ISABELLE takes a jellaba and puts it on, slowly, formally. Freeze while she is doing this. Once in it, she feels as at home in it as JENNY obviously feels awkward.)*

NATALIE. And they gave me this in secret. *(She takes out a captain's uniform.)*

ANTOINE. Someone they killed probably. They have no respect for human life. You see how dangerous they are.

ISABELLE. "Always behave as if you were going to die immediately." Remember when we were Stoics and we tried to live in that barrel for a month?

NATALIE *(going over to JENNY and putting a "feminine" scarf over her head)*. I'm afraid reading is a hereditary disease in our family. I would keep books well away from your children when they're young, otherwise it's very hard to wean them from all that nonsense when they're older. If only we could get her married, she'd forget all those books, but it's the quotes that drive men away. I'm glad Antoine, at least, is saved. *(As NATALIE is saying this ISABELLE is putting the captain's jacket on YASMINA. ISABELLE and YASMINA giggle, YASMINA doing a military stance. JENNY suddenly notices them.)*

JENNY. Don't do that, it's…blasphemy.

ISABELLE. Why, do you think clothes make the monk?

ANTOINE. Isabelle looks like all our recruits. No one would know you were a girl. Is this male or female? *(He puts on a jellaba, joining in the game.)*

JENNY. If anyone sees us, we'll be ruined.

ISABELLE *(to ANTOINE)*. Let's go to those dark dens in the Arab quarter and have a smoke.

ANTOINE. If they recognize us…*(Throat-slitting gesture.)*

ISABELLE. We'll say we're from Tunis. That'll explain my accent.

JENNY. You can't go out. What about me?

ISABELLE. Come, Antoine, for at least one evening, let's go back to our dreams.

NATALIE. I want you to come with me to the market.

ISABELLE. I told you I won't help you cheat those people any more.

NATALIE. I'm only trying to save some money.

ISABELLE. One evening, Antoine. *(They begin to go.)*

JENNY. Ooooh—ooooh my stomach. I think I'm going to faint. Don't leave me, Antoine.

ISABELLE. You have Natalie and the "captain."

JENNY. Oooh. *(Doubles over.)* Put your hands on my forehead, Antoine. It's the only thing that'll help.

ISABELLE. Why don't you just tell him you want him to stay instead of acting ill, hypocrite?

NATALIE. Don't upset a pregnant woman, Isabelle.

ISABELLE. Antoine...*(ANTOINE goes over to JENNY and puts his hands on her forehead. ISABELLE turns to leave.)*

NATALIE. What are you doing?

ISABELLE. I'm going outside.

NATALIE. A woman can't go out by herself at this time of night.

ISABELLE. But in these...I'm not a woman.

SCENE FIVE

The Kasbah. ISABELLE, alone.

ISABELLE. If, down an obscure alleyway, a voice shouts at me: hey you, shopkeeper—I'll not turn around. If the voice pursues me: foreigner, European—I'll not turn around. If the voice says: you, woman, yes, woman—I'll not turn around, no, I'll not even turn my head. Even when it whispers, Isabelle, Isabelle Eberhardt—

even then I won't turn around. But if it hails me: you
there, who need vast spaces and ask for nothing but to
move, you, alone, free, seeking peace and a home in
the desert, who wish only to obey the strange ciphers of
your fate—yes, then I will turn around, then I'll answer: I am here: Si Mahmoud.

SCENE SIX

*The desert, ISABELLE, SALEH and BOU SAADI are
sitting passing around a pipe full of kif. They are very
stoned, from lack of food and the hashish. Long si-
lences, then rapid bursts of speech. The poetry must not
be "recited." For the Arabs, it is their natural form of
speech.*

SALEH. "The warrior was brave. Alas the beautiful young
    man fell. He shone like silver. Now he is in Paradise,
    free from all troubles."
ISABELLE. Was he fighting the Tidjanis, Saleh?
SALEH. No, Si Mahmoud, that is a song against the
    French. *(Silence.)*
ISABELLE. Tell me more about the wise men.
SALEH. Usually they're sheikhs who have been handed
    their knowledge by their fathers and then give it to a
    son. They live in the monasteries. We'll stay in one
    tomorrow.
BOU SAADI. But sometimes they wander and look just
    like beggars.
SALEH. There used to be very many, but the French are
    getting rid of them.

BOU SAADI. You must be careful what you say against the French, Saleh, it was God's will they become our rulers, it was written.

SALEH. Have we read it badly? *(Silence.)*

BOU SAADI. One of the most famous marabouts used to live not far from here. Lalla Zineb. Many people visit her tomb.

ISABELLE. A woman?

BOU SAADI. Not an ordinary woman.

ISABELLE. But a woman?

SALEH. What difference does it make, Si Mahmoud, if she was wise? They say she predicted the victory of the French and then died of grief. *(Silence.)* If it is wisdom you seek, Si Mahmoud, you should spend some time in the monasteries. We could take you to the one where the leader of our sect lives.

ISABELLE. And you my friends, what have you found in the desert?

SALEH. I had a cousin who had a beautiful white mare. She was fast, exquisite. He'd had her since he was a boy. She was his treasure and his love. One night, she disappeared. He searched for months and found her at last in the camp of a few Tidjanis. He waited until the night to get her back, but someone must have seen him because he stumbled on her body on his way to the camp. Her throat had been slit, his beautiful white mare. Some time later he managed to kill the man who had stolen her. It's only fair, a mare is more valuable than a wife to us. But the Tidjanis told the French about it. They're very friendly with the French. He was judged in the city and then sent away to forced labour in a place called Corsica. Very few men come back

from Corsica and then only to die. That's the law of the
French.

BOU SAADI. We were born crossing the desert, but now
we have to ask permission to go to certain places.

ISABELLE. Was it better always to fight the Tidjanis?

SALEH. It was our custom. *(Silence.)*

"She said to me:

Why are your tears so white?

I answered:

Beloved, I have cried so long my tears are as white
as my hair."

ISABELLE. One day we'll understand, Saleh.

SALEH. Ah, Si Mahmoud, perhaps you will, you're
learned.

BOU SAADI. We'll leave a few hours before dawn. I
hope you're not feeling too weak, Si Mahmoud.

ISABELLE. No, my friends, but why didn't you tell me to
bring food? I've eaten all of yours.

BOU SAADI. We're used to this life.

SALEH. "She said to me:

Why are your tears black?

I answered:

I have no more tears, those are my pupils…"

(CAPTAIN SOUBIEL enters.)

CAPTAIN. You there, who are you and where are you
going? *(BOU SAADI and SALEH jump up, acting in-
creasingly stupid as the CAPTAIN stares at them. BOU
SAADI in particular almost caricatures "oriental ser-
vility.")*

BOU SAADI. We're traders on our way to El-Oued, Allah
willing.

CAPTAIN. Don't give me any of this Allah business. The three of you are traders?

BOU SAADI. This is a young Tunisian student on his way to the monasteries down south.

CAPTAIN. Monasteries, we've just had a report on those monasteries. Fortresses, that's what they are, hotbeds of resistance. All those sheikhs with their wives and slaves pretending to teach religion when they're shouting propaganda against the French. Don't talk to me about monasteries. *(Stares at ISABELLE.)* A Tunisian student, we've had a report about that too. You're not very dark.

BOU SAADI. Men from the city are lighter than us. Much sun in the Sahara.

CAPTAIN. Can't he speak for himself? What's your name?

ISABELLE. Si Mahmoud.

CAPTAIN. Si Mahmoud. You two, go make some tea.

BOU SAADI. We have no tea.

CAPTAIN. Well, then, go have a piss and don't come back until I call you. Stay where I can see you and you, stay here. *(Has a good stare and then becomes extremely courteous.)* Remarkable, I must say, remarkable. I wouldn't have known. I'm honoured. You've become a legend in the Legion: it's one thing to go out looking for some Arab scum criminal, but a mysterious young lady...

ISABELLE. My name is Si Mahmoud.

CAPTAIN. You can of course rely on the honour of the French Army to keep your secret. Ha, ha, you Russian girls are extraordinary. One of them blew up the Tsar or his cousin the other day and now we have this young thing living it out with the Arabs. They say Dostoevsky does this to you, gives you a taste for cockroaches. But, mademoiselle, if you wished to see the country, you should have come to us. We would be only too pleased to escort you and you would find our company much more entertaining than that of those sandfleas.

ISABELLE. You shouldn't speak of the Arabs in that manner, Captain. They resent it.

CAPTAIN. You must tell me how to run the country, mademoiselle. It'll pass the time as we travel. Dunes get monotonous.

ISABELLE. I am travelling with my friends, Captain.

CAPTAIN. What? Are there more of you? Do we have a whole boarding school of romantic young girls?

ISABELLE. My friends Saleh and Bou Saadi.

CAPTAIN. She calls these dregs of humanity friends. Ah, youth, the female heart. I admire your spirit, mademoiselle, but it is the duty of the French Army to rescue damsels in distress.

ISABELLE. My friends will look after me.

CAPTAIN. Mademoiselle, I'm here to protect you. These people smile at you one day and cut your throat the next. You see, they have no logic, no French education. And if they ever found out... You're not at all bad looking you know.

ISABELLE. I choose to travel with them.

CAPTAIN. You're quite a brave little character. I like that. I think we'll get on very well. You remind me of a delightfully unbroken young filly.

ISABELLE. Whereas you, Captain, remind me of a heavy cascade of camel piss. Mind you, nothing wrong with camel piss, I just don't choose to have it on top of me. Or to put it another way, I'd rather kiss the open mouth of a Maccabean corpse dead of the Asiatic cholera than "travel" with you, Captain. *(Freeze.)*

CAPTAIN. May I see your papers?

ISABELLE. What papers?

CAPTAIN. You must have government permission to travel through French territory.

ISABELLE. This is the desert. It's free.

CAPTAIN. This is French territory, under the rule of law and civilization and we require even sluts to have the correct papers. I'm waiting. I see you have no papers. You there...*(BOU SAADI and SALEH come back.)* Do you know what this friend of yours Si Mahmoud is?

ISABELLE. Captain, the honour of the French Army.

CAPTAIN. We save the honour of our own kind. You'll kick yourselves when you find out. This little Tunisian friend of yours, ha, ha...

ISABELLE. Captain, please.

CAPTAIN. This Si Mahmoud is a woman. *(Silence. BOU SAADI laughs stupidly. SALEH doesn't react at all.)* Look under her clothes if you don't believe me.

SALEH *(slowly)*. Si Mahmoud has a very good knowledge of medicine. He's helped people with their eyes and cured children.

CAPTAIN. Probably told them to wash. It's a woman I tell you. You must be stupider than I thought not to have noticed or at least asked a few questions.

SALEH. It is a courtesy in our country not to be curious about the stranger. We accept whatever name Si Mahmoud wishes to give us.

ISABELLE. You knew.

SALEH. We heard. We chose not to believe it. *(To the CAPTAIN.)* Si Mahmoud knows the Koran better than we do. He's in search of wisdom. We wish to help him.

CAPTAIN. Wisdom? That's the story she's spreading. I think it's more like information to pass on to people who don't belong here, like the English. They're always using women for this sort of thing. They can't forgive us for having produced Joan of Arc. You have ten days to bring this agitator back to the city. You know what happens if you don't.

ISABELLE. I'll appeal.

CAPTAIN. Yes, in Paris. It's never wise to refuse the protection of the French Army. A good journey. *(He leaves.)*

ISABELLE. I'm doing no harm...

BOU SAADI. It's not a good idea to irritate Europeans. It's best to pretend you're stupid and keep laughing. I'm very good at it. Saleh is learning very slowly.

ISABELLE. I want nothing to do with these people. Why won't they let me alone? Ah, my friends, it's written I must leave you, but I'll come back, I'll come back.

SONG 2
(Optional)

VERDA MILES as a colonial soldier.

ACT TWO

SCENE ONE

A salon in Paris, VERDA MILES, SEVERINE, LYDIA, EUGENIE, ISABELLE, and PASHA, a servant.

SONG 3

VERDA MILES, an English male impersonator, is singing a music hall song...

LYDIA. Isn't she extraordinary? Do you know I am almost in love with that man about town. And it was so kind of her to come and sing for my little salon.

EUGENIE. Ah, but your salon, such a setting for an artist.

SEVERINE. Don't be a hypocrite, Lydia. She knows everyone is at your little salon. And I've been invited tonight because you want me to write a story on her.

LYDIA. What she is doing is so important—for us.

SEVERINE. Lots of women have gone on stage dressed as men. It shows off their figures.

LYDIA. When Verda Miles is on stage, she *is* a man.

EUGENIE. And "man is the measure of all things."

LYDIA. Do interview her, Severine.

SEVERINE. You can't interview English people, they don't know how to talk about themselves.

(PASHA comes in with a tray of champagne.)

SEVERINE. I say, is that real?

LYDIA. No, it's just Jean. But the clothes are real. I had them copied from the *Arabian Nights.*

SEVERINE. The Countess Holst has one, a genuine one, but he's not as convincing.

LYDIA. And she had to sleep with the Turkish Ambassador to get him.

EUGENIE. When I was in Cairo I thought of bringing one back with me, but it's cruel to take them out of their natural environment.

LYDIA. Why don't I engage Verda Miles in conversation? You can simply listen.

SEVERINE. You'll make it too philosophical and I'll miss the story—if there is one.

LYDIA. My dear, you can't talk philosophy with English women, they think it's something naughty their husbands did as boys. No, I'll start with dogs.

EUGENIE *(seeing ISABELLE).* Lydia, what do I see? Ah, there, there is a true one, I can tell. A young oriental prince, look at the simplicity, the dignity. Oh, do present him to us.

SEVERINE. It's even an Arab who looks a little like Rimbaud, the Countess will be green when I tell her. How very clever of you.

LYDIA. Yes, that's quite a find, but that's not a real Arab either. Much more interesting, you have there a young woman who travels with the savage tribes in the Sahara. Her name's Isabelle Eberhardt. Russian, I think, she won't talk much about herself.

SEVERINE. Eberhardt's a Jewish name.

LYDIA. Yes, well, they're all nomads, aren't they? She had some troubles with officials in North Africa and

she's come to Paris to ask the French Government to
help her. She's very naïve.

SEVERINE. She must be to think the Government will
help anyone. Does she have enough money to bribe
them?

LYDIA. She seems to have left everything behind—some-
where.

EUGENIE. The nomadic spirit, it's so noble, so carefree.

LYDIA. She knows almost no one here, but look at her,
she could become quite the rage. You might help her. I
believe she writes.

SEVERINE. Oh dear, descriptions of the sunset in sub-
Wordsworthian rhymes. So many interesting people
would still be remembered if they hadn't left behind
their memoirs. *(LYDIA has been waving ISABELLE
over.)*

LYDIA. Pasha, more champagne please.

SEVERINE *(courteous, intrigued).* Would you like some
champagne, mademoiselle?

ISABELLE. Is that what it is? It's good, I've had six
glasses already.

EUGENIE *(with an exaggerated Arab salutation, or an
attempt at one).* I am so delighted. I too have been
there. *(ISABELLE stares blankly.)* Why didn't we dis-
cover it before? All those trips to Athens and Rome
staring at ruins when we had the real thing all the time
in the Orient. *(ISABELLE chokes on her drink, coughs
and spits.)*

ISABELLE. Oh, forgot, used to the sand. Sorry, Lydia.

EUGENIE. The Homeric gesture, is that not so? *(To the
OTHERS.)* You can't imagine what it's like to see lying
in the sun, or mending shoes, men of such consular

types, all clad in white like the senators of Rome. Each
one with the mien of a Cato or a Brutus.

LYDIA. There's Verda, excellent. *(Champagne. ISA-
BELLE drinks another glass.)*

VERDA. No, I never drink. *(To ISABELLE.)* What a
charming costume you have.

EUGENIE. The flowing simplicity of the African garb, so
free, so...Athenian.

VERDA. I'd like to copy it. You see. I have an idea for a
new song, it would be an oriental melody, exotic, and
with that costume...

ISABELLE. It's not a costume, it's my clothes.

VERDA. Of course, that's what I meant. Do you know
any oriental songs?

EUGENIE. Those oriental melodies—so biblical.

ISABELLE *(very flat)*. Darling, I love you, darling, I
adore you, exactly like to—maaa—to sauce. When I
saw you there there there on the balcony, I thought...
(Hiccups.) That's all I know.

LYDIA. They have the most beautiful breed of hounds in
Egypt. They're called Ibizan hounds...

ISABELLE. I ate some cat in Tunisia. They said it was
rabbit, but I could tell it was cat, I found a claw. It
tasted all right.

EUGENIE. I found them so admirable in the simplicity of
their needs. A population of Socrates.

LYDIA. What made you decide to sing men's songs, Miss
Miles?

VERDA. I started singing on the stage when I was three
and at the age of six I had run through most of the
female repertoire. By the time I was seven I thought I
would have to retire. But then, one night, I noticed by
chance—if there is such a thing as chance—my father's

hat and cape hanging over the back of a chair. You see my father was also in the music-hall, as was my mother, who was Scottish. That is, her father was Scottish. As I was saying, I saw the hat and cape and put them on. I went to the mirror and when I saw myself I suddenly had hundreds of exciting roles before me. I've been a male impersonator ever since. It is, how shall I saw, much more interesting, much more challenging to play men. There is more variety...more...

LYDIA. More scope. How well I understand you. I myself occasionally scribble. Oh, not professionally, like Severine, not writings I would necessarily show. Although, of course, if Severine did ask to see them, I might, just as a friend...Do you know that in order to write seriously I must dress as a man? I finally understood why: when I am dressed as a woman, like this, I find I am most concerned with the silky sound of my skirt rustling on the floor, or I spend hours watching the lace fall over my wrist, white against white. But when I dress as a man, I simply begin to think, I get ideas. I'm sure that's why Severine is such a brilliant journalist, she always dresses as a man.

SEVERINE. My dear Lydia, you know perfectly well I wear male clothes so I can take my girlfriends to coffee bars without having men pester us.

VERDA (nervous). Of course I never have that sort of problem because I am always with my husband. And I love to wear women's clothes. My husband says I am the most womanly woman he has ever known.

SEVERINE. Lydia was quite falling in love with your man about town.

VERDA. It's puzzling how many letters I get from women, young girls even. Sometimes they are so passionate they make me blush. One girl quite pursued me. She sent flowers to my dressing room and every time I performed I would see her, up close, staring at me. It was most disturbing. And her letters! At last, I had to invite her to my dressing room. I let my hair all the way down and wore the most feminine gown I could find. And then I gave her a good talking to. She never came back.

SEVERINE. Have men never written you love letters?

VERDA. Yes, but that's different. That's normal.

SEVERINE. Normality, the golden cage. And we poor banished species trail around, looking through the bars, wishing we were in there. But we're destined for the curiosity shops, labelled as the weird mistakes of nature, the moment of God's hesitation between Adam and Eve, anatomical convolutions, our souls inside out and alone, always alone, outside those bars. Do you love normality, Miss Miles?

EUGENIE. I was never considered normal. At school, my dancing master said my feet were perfect examples of the evils of anarchy. My deportment had revolutionary tendencies and the sound of my voice, I was told, was more raucous than the Communist Manifesto. No amount of hours spent practising in front of empty chairs taught me how to engage a young man in conversation and at last my poor parents said in despair, let her travel. I have not been unhappy, but I would have liked to be useful, or at least a philologist.

LYDIA. I think normality is a fashion. Here we are, five women and four of us are dressed as men. And I'm only wearing skirts because there are some German diplomats here and they're very sticky about these things. I believe the century we're entering will see a revolution greater even than the French revolution. They defrocked the priests, we'll defrock the women.

VERDA. We'll lose all our strength.

SEVERINE. Tell us about the desert, Miss Eberhardt.

ISABELLE. Sand.

LYDIA. Can't you help her, Severine?

SEVERINE. Do you remember the Marquis de Mores?

LYDIA. Spanish? Stood around looking passionate? With an American wife? He hasn't been seen in ages.

SEVERINE. He was killed down there. His wife—you know what Americans are like—has taken it very personally. She wants the French government to find out what happened. It seems they're showing a most unusual lack of curiosity. *(To ISABELLE.)* We might persuade her to send you down there to collect some information. I'd like to go myself. I smell a story which might be quite embarrassing to some people. We could travel together. I'd enjoy that.

ISABELLE. Do you really like women?

SEVERINE *(seductive)*. Have you lived in the Orient and remained a prude?

ISABELLE. Me? Ha!

SEVERINE. There are thousands of women in this city who would do anything to be made love to by me. But I like women with character.

ISABELLE. I'm not a woman. I'm Si Mahmoud. I like men. They like me. As a boy, I mean. And I have a firm rule: no Europeans up my arse. *(Freeze.)*

VERDA. I really must go. My husband...

ISABELLE. Did I say something wrong?

EUGENIE. The nomadic turn of phrase: so childlike.

SEVERINE. I don't like vulgarity. I'm afraid I can't help you.

ISABELLE. You look just like Captain Soubiel now. He wanted to "protect me." And there was something to protect then. *(Drinks, hopeless.)* I spent nine months working on the docks of Marseilles to pay for this trip. Loading ships.

SEVERINE. Too bad it was a waste.

ISABELLE. Yeah, it was written. Too free with my tongue. Too free. *(She drinks another glass and passes out.)*

LYDIA. I'll have to teach her some manners. I'm sorry.

SEVERINE. That spirit isn't for corsets. Look at her. She's younger than I am and she probably has malaria, who knows what else. Nine months loading ships— that's the work of ex-convicts. What a story.

LYDIA. She's ruined everything tonight.

SEVERINE. I'm not sure…No, I'll help her. *(The melancholic sound of an Arab love song…)*

SCENE TWO

A zouaia (monastery) in the desert. SI LACHMI, SALEH, BOU SAADI and ISABELLE.

ISABELLE *(slightly out of it)*. Oh, these happy, these drunken hours of return.

BOU SAADI *(to SI LACHMI)*. It was written Si Mahmoud would come back to us.

SALEH. He can now become one of us, a Qadria.

ISABELLE. I wanted to possess this country. It has possessed me.

SI LACHMI. There are at least a hundred different Sufi orders but the Qadria is one of the oldest.

ISABELLE. I've been in such a hurry to live.

SI LACHMI. We are also the most numerous.

SALEH. There are more of us than Tidjanis.

SI LACHMI. You will have twenty thousand brothers.

ISABELLE. The senses have tormented me.

BOU SAADI. The Qadrias are bound by links of affection.

SALEH. And solidarity, limitless devotion.

ISABELLE. A certain languor in these sands.

SI LACHMI. You'll be safe in our territories.

ISABELLE. Take off at last the grimacing, degraded mask.

SI LACHMI. All our monasteries are open to you.

ISABELLE. This is my property: the extended horizon.

SI LACHMI Keep this chaplet, it'll protect you.

ISABELLE. The luxurious decor of the dunes: mine.

SI LACHMI. There is no dogma. We believe only in the equality of all men and gentleness of heart. You must also show absolute obedience to your sheikh. Our founder, Abd-el-Qader was most loved for his friendship with the oppressed. He loathed hypocrisy, all lies. You must be generous and show pity to all.

ISABELLE. And wisdom?

SI LACHMI. That comes later, Si Mahmoud. You're still young. Free yourself first from the vulgarity of the world.

ISABELLE. Doesn't the word Sufi come from the Greek *sofos,* wise?

SI LACHMI. It comes from a Berber word that means to excel. But that isn't important. Try to be a brave and good man, that's all we ask. (*Pause. In a different tone.*) So you have been visiting France?

SALEH. Si Mahmoud has been asked to find the murderers of a European called the Marquis de Mores.

ISABELLE. Oh yes, I'd forgotten. He was an explorer.

SI LACHMI. The *French* have asked you to look for his murderers?

ISABELLE. Not exactly the French. His wife.

SI LACHMI. Indeed.

ISABELLE. She gave me a lot of money. I should make an effort. Why would anyone want to murder an explorer?

SI LACHMI. He himself was not French?

ISABELLE. I don't think so. Why?

SI LACHMI. I am fascinated by the European tribal wars. They are more bitter than ours, but are conducted with much more subtlety. I am learning much from them.

SALEH. We kill people we don't like openly, in battle.

ISABELLE. You think it was the French themselves who wanted to get rid of him?

SI LACHMI. God alone knows the hearts of men. Do the French know with what purpose you've come back?

ISABELLE. I don't hide anything. I'm not a hypocrite.

SI LACHMI. We don't forbid prudence, Si Mahmoud.

SALEH. You're our brother now. We'll help you.

ISABELLE. If Allah's willing I'll find the murderers, if not—then I suppose it's not written they should be found. Does poverty allow the possession of a horse?

SI LACHMI. We don't deny pleasure. Each follows his own capacities.

(During this last exchange, the MURDERER comes in, unseen. He strikes with a sabre. ISABELLE turns just in time to avert it and only her arm is struck. The MURDERER is caught by SALEH and BOU SAADI.)

SI LACHMI. What's your name, you dog?

BOU SAADI. That's a Muslim brother. Do you know what you've done?

SI LACHMI. What's your name?

SALEH. Who ordered you to do this?

MURDERER. Allah.

SI LACHMI. God told you to kill a brother?

MURDERER. That's a woman.

SI LACHMI. It's no business of yours who this person is if we accept him as our brother. You question a sheikh?

MURDERER. Allah ordered me to kill that person who offends our law.

SI LACHMI. What law, fool? My sisters dressed as young men when they travelled. Who are you to judge? Who told you to do this?

MURDERER. Allah.

SALEH. Or the Tidjanis, or the French? (*SI LACHMI hands the sabre to ISABELLE.*)

SI LACHMI. You may kill him. (*ISABELLE seizes the sabre, then stops herself.*)

ISABELLE. Why? (*Gentle.*) Have I offended you without knowing?

MURDERER. You have done nothing to me, but if I have another chance, I'll kill you.

ISABELLE. Strange...I don't hate you. No, I forgive you. But I did you no harm.

MURDERER. You're offending our customs.

ISABELLE. But that's why I left *them*. (*Throws the sabre down.*) No, you're an instrument, but why? A riddle... Brothers, if it was written that I must die...But so young, without understanding...no. I can't die in this silence. Don't let me die here. Don't let me disappear, without a trace. Who wants to do this to me?

SCENE THREE

The courtroom in Constantine. ISABELLE and the MURDERER. As the MURDERER speaks, he changes into the JUDGE.

MURDERER/JUDGE. "An angel appeared to tell me the Marabout of the Qadrias, Si Lachmi, would be proceeding to El-Oued accompanied by Miss Eberhardt who called herself Si Mahmoud and wore masculine dress, thus making trouble in our religion." This, Miss Eberhardt, is what the accused has to say in his defence. Have you anything to add?

ISABELLE. There is no law in the Muslim religion that says a woman may not dress as a man.

JUDGE. There should be. It's unChristian. Why do you wear it?

ISABELLE. It's practical for riding.

JUDGE. Women have traditionally ridden in dresses.

ISABELLE. Side-saddle! Imagine me joining a Qadria charge riding side-saddle. I'm greatly admired for my riding.

JUDGE. Did you say you joined a battle, Miss Eberhardt?

ISABELLE *(modestly)*. Just a small raid. The sun was rising, it seemed covered in blood. There were about a hundred of us and...

JUDGE. Who were you fighting?

ISABELLE. Must have been the Tidjanis.

JUDGE. I hope it was not the French, Miss Eberhardt.

ISABELLE. No, no...

JUDGE. You've been heard to complain against the French.

ISABELLE. France could help this country so much, with medicine, technical knowledge. But for some reason it's making the people here worse off than they already are. The Arabs will soon hate the French even more... *(Stops herself.)*

JUDGE. You seem very friendly with the Arabs.

ISABELLE. I'm a Qadria, that's why I'm sure the murderer is a Tidjani and was paid to kill me. I don't want him punished too severely, but if he gets away with it, I'll no longer be safe.

JUDGE. Why don't you return to Europe?

ISABELLE. I belong here.

JUDGE. Are you not a European?

ISABELLE. No, that is, not now...

JUDGE. You were born in Europe, Miss Eberhardt, you are also a young woman.

ISABELLE. I'm not...*(Stops herself.)* I belong in the desert.

JUDGE. These are troubled times...

ISABELLE. I'm not doing any harm.

JUDGE. You've already driven a simple, ordinary Muslim to madness by your behavior, Miss Eberhardt. If only these people were civilized, we could allow your wanderings.

ISABELLE. You don't want me to travel?

JUDGE. We must ask you to refrain from visiting places where your presence might cause an unpleasant incident.

ISABELLE. I'll stay in Si Lachmi's monastery.

JUDGE. We particularly do not want you in the monasteries.

ISABELLE. I'll travel further south.

JUDGE. Miss Eberhardt, we feel your presence would be a provocation anywhere in the desert.

ISABELLE. Oh, no, oh, please.

JUDGE. I'm sorry to put an end to your gallivantings.

ISABELLE. You—it's you. You've been trying to get rid of me all along.

JUDGE. We're trying to establish order.

ISABELLE. You're terrified of me! Your order is so fragile.

JUDGE. May I point out, Miss Eberhardt, that a man was recently sent to prison in England for a much lesser offence than yours.

ISABELLE. What? He took a walk on the beach?

JUDGE. This Mr. Wilde had a perversion of inclination. You, Miss Eberhardt, have perverted nature.

ISABELLE. You mean nature as farmed by you to make you fat.

JUDGE. We will of course imprison your assailant.

ISABELLE. My friends, my brothers, where are my friends?

JUDGE. But you're to stay out of the desert. For good.

ISABELLE. Fenced out. Always!

SEVERINE. Fenced in, Isabelle, all of us.

SCENE FOUR

ISABELLE and SEVERINE.

ISABELLE. Blocked. Detour. Blocked again. Need some absinthe. Buy me an absinthe, girl scribe.

SEVERINE. I thought Muslims didn't drink.

ISABELLE. Shouldn't. Do. Have you seen how supple Arabic writing is? Not like that French print. Need

some absinthe. Si Mahmoud is dying of thirst. Hang on
my every word, steal my story and won't give me to
drink. European!

SEVERINE. I'm trying to keep you sober for Colonel
Lyautey. It would help if you made sense.

ISABELLE. Make better sense with absinthe. Understand
the world then: nice blurr. "Alas my soul for youth
that's gone."

SEVERINE. You're twenty-seven!

ISABELLE. Lived fast. Too many detours and had to run.

SEVERINE. Here comes the Colonel. Try to behave yourself.

ISABELLE. The French: camel piss. I forgive them.

SEVERINE. He's an exception. The Arabs like him.

ISABELLE. Europe has taught them ignorance.

SEVERINE. Isabelle—it's your last chance.

(COLONEL LYAUTEY enters.)

SEVERINE. Colonel. I've heard so much about you.

LYAUTEY. And I about you, Severine: your pen strikes
more terror in the heart of the French government than
the rattle of the Arab sabre.

ISABELLE. His speech jingles like his medals.

SEVERINE. Colonel, you wished to meet Isabelle
Eberhardt.

LYAUTEY *(bows)*. Si Mahmoud.

ISABELLE. My sister married a dandelion. I was courted
by his brother, a radish, no, his cousin, an orchid, and
here's a multicoloured bouquet of medals bowing before me. The grace of Allah follow your footsteps, master. *(Bows down to the ground.)* A drop of absinthe for
the poet's soul, Colonel, to remember Paradise.

SEVERINE. Colonel, you must excuse her—she's been so
  badly treated.

LYAUTEY. I've wanted to meet you for some time, Si
  Mahmoud.

ISABELLE. Yeah, I'm famous. All bad. They hate me.
  Why?

LYAUTEY. Bloodthirsty mercenaries defend the bound-
  aries of convention, Si Mahmoud, and your escape was
  too flamboyant. You remind me of the young Arab
  warrior who wears bright colours so he'll be seen first
  by the enemy.

ISABELLE. Ah, you're the firing squad. Here. *(Points to
  her heart, spreads her arms.)* Scribe, take down the
  martyr's last words: Si Mahmoud, heart without guile,
  dies, crossed by European civilization...

SEVERINE. Colonel, I'm sorry...

LYAUTEY. It's all right. I like refractory spirits.

ISABELLE. Why do compliments in French always sound
  translated? I hate flowers, that's why I like the desert.
  Barred by the hedges now. Are you very brave, Colonel, to have picked so many medals?

LYAUTEY. Yes, Si Mahmoud, and so, I'm told, are you.

ISABELLE. With me bravery is a languor of the instincts.
  Are you languid, Colonel?

SEVERINE. Isabelle, stop playing.

ISABELLE. Why? Travelling show: examine here the
  monstrous folds of uncorseted nature, the pervert seed
  that would not flourish on European manure. Complete
  with witty and scientific commentary by our own
  Sevvy the Scribe, straight from Paris...

SEVERINE. It's hopeless, we had better go.

LYAUTEY. Wait. Si Mahmoud, I don't like hedges either.
  I come from Provence: it's dry there and barren. And

you can still hear in the walls the echoes of chivalry and nobility, what you have here, what we're destroying.

ISABELLE. I believed in French civilization once. Is it the climate that makes it rot?

LYAUTEY. The wrong ones came. You used to travel with the Qadrias.

SEVERINE. Isabelle can go places where no other European would be safe.

LYAUTEY. Do you want to travel again?

ISABELLE. When I came out of hospital after my wound, the dunes had shrivelled. I wondered if they'd been empty all the time.

SEVERINE. You were ill. You know you want to travel.

ISABELLE. "Anywhere, anywhere as long as it's out of this world." Let the cloud of oriental perfume that was my soul vanish. No trace.

LYAUTEY. They say, Si Mahmoud, you're a young man in search of knowledge.

ISABELLE. Was.

SEVERINE. She's accepted by all the marabouts. It's only the French who prevent her from returning.

LYAUTEY. My predecessors have a lot to answer for. (*To ISABELLE.*) The Zianya sect is known for its pious and disinterested leaders. The Qadria have great respect for the Zianya.

ISABELLE. How do you know all this?

LYAUTEY. You forget, I love this country.

ISABELLE. "The tongue is a man's one half."

LYAUTEY. "The other the heart within." And who can judge the heart? Have you heard of the Zianya leader, Sidi Brahim?

ISABELLE. Even our marabouts look up to him.

LYAUTEY. Would you like to visit his school?

ISABELLE. Can't. It's in Morocco.

LYAUTEY. I can get you in.

ISABELLE. Is it written that Si Mahmoud shall speak to Sidi Brahim, that wisdom might be gained at last?

LYAUTEY. What will you need?

ISABELLE. A good horse.

LYAUTEY. When can you leave?

ISABELLE. Tomorrow.

SEVERINE. Morocco. She'll never come back, Colonel.

LYAUTEY. You can only stay five months this first time, Si Mahmoud. Please tell Sidi Brahim the French will help him if he wishes to extricate himself from his enemies.

SEVERINE. I see. The conquest of Morocco.

LYAUTEY. Not this time, I hope. But Si Mahmoud will tell you that country is devastated by marauding tribes.

ISABELLE. Too much bloodshed, yes.

LYAUTEY. We would help, no more.

SEVERINE. Shall we call it then the digestion of Morocco?

LYAUTEY. I'll expect you in Ain-Sefra in five months, Si Mahmoud, and then we'll have long chats about this country. How did my predecessors not appreciate you?

ISABELLE. From the point of view of bread and Swiss cheese, the love of the desert is an unhealthy appetite.

LYAUTEY. What idiots not to have understood you. Poor Si Mahmoud.

ISABELLE. Poor Si Mahmoud.

SEVERINE. She loves pity, Colonel.

ISABELLE. We Slavs are like that. We love the knout and then we love being pitied for having suffered the knout. And you, chronicler, must make no judgments. We souls of the desert *(Hiccups.)* love the knout.

LYAUTEY. Five months then. Your word of honour. I'll find a way of thanking you, Severine.

SEVERINE. It may be too late, Colonel, you should have found her before.

LYAUTEY. They should have found me before. It may be too late for me too. Territories exploding, violence sowed and reaped, so unnecessary. Only you, Severine, it's not too late for you.

ISABELLE. It's never too late for the chroniclers.

SEVERINE. But that's not what you meant, Colonel, is it?

LYAUTEY. No.

SCENE FIVE

Ain-Sefra. Same as the first scene, a few hours later. ISABELLE and SEVERINE.

ISABELLE. Very strict at the monastery. Walk towards the gate and a shadow bars your path. But Sidi Brahim let me pace. He understood Si Mahmoud had been too often locked in. His son lived in another quarter. There were many young men of great beauty in those rooms, and we don't hate love. But I couldn't join. They would know I was not completely a man, and also, much of that was gone. Slowly, slowly, the torment of the senses opens to the modulation of the dunes. Only a ripple here and there betrays the passage of the storm. Sidi Brahim wanted me to go further south and describe the country to the Colonel.

SEVERINE. Why didn't you?

ISABELLE. Promised I'd come here.

SEVERINE. You had more than a month left.

ISABELLE. If a man be old and a fool...suddenly, suddenly Si Mahmoud felt a shiver of fear. Suddenly my destiny: forgot the script. So I thought I'll come back, word of honour, and Si Mahmoud is important now, not broken.

SEVERINE. Shouldn't you get some rest? You must be coherent if you're seeing the Colonel later.

ISABELLE. Always coherent. It's the letters that get scrambled.

SEVERINE. I must go in. I feel faint.

ISABELLE. Hard work chronicling. Kept you up all night unravelling the Mektoub. Rest. Will you write my story? Practical guide for girls with unhealthy desires. With diagrams for the Europeans, the Cartesians. They couldn't fence in my tongue. Poor Sevvy, sweet scribe of unCartesian appetites, rebuild your dream.

SEVERINE. Will you find your way?

ISABELLE. Stay outside, head against stone and the soul more pure. If a man be old...but a young man may yet cast off his foolishness. I'm not wise, I'm not wise. *(Feels something, sticks out her hand.)* Rain? It doesn't rain in the desert. Mirage. No, rain, that's nice. Sleep in the rain. What's that noise?

SEVERINE. Thunder probably. There have been storms in the mountains. Don't wander off.

ISABELLE. Make my report to the Colonel, then wander off. Tell them Si Mahmoud...*(But SEVERINE has left.)* The rain. Get clean that way, wash the traces and the letters. Fresh sand, new letters. *(She lies down.)*

SCENE SIX

Ain-Sefra. SEVERINE, COLONEL LYAUTEY and the JUDGE.

SEVERINE. Drowned!

LYAUTEY. We came too late.

SEVERINE. Drowned in Ain-Sefra.

JUDGE. In the middle of the desert? That's no place to drown.

SEVERINE. A flash flood. The whole native quarter washed away.

LYAUTEY. My men rushed down. We couldn't find her.

JUDGE. It's said she didn't even try to save herself.

SEVERINE. Our rebel warrior, Colonel.

JUDGE. Close the file. This person must be officially forgotten.

LYAUTEY. We found some journals. Would you like to see them, Severine?

SEVERINE. With pleasure. *(They walk off, arm in arm. Lights fade to blackout.)*

END

DIRECTOR'S NOTES

DIRECTOR'S NOTES

DIRECTOR'S NOTES

DIRECTOR'S NOTES